TINGGUIANS

Merlina Espiritu Salamanca,
LL.B., Ed.S.

To order additional copies of this book, contact:
Xlibris
844-714-8691
www.Xlibris.com
Orders@Xlibris.com

THE PRIDE OF THE TINGGUIANS
PRIVATE FAMILY COLLECTION
DANGLAS, ABRA, PHILIPPINES

BY

Merlina Espiritu Salamanca, LL.B., Ed.S.

"APPRECIATING AND SUPPORTING GLOBAL CULTURAL AWARENESS
BY SHARING CULTURAL HERITAGE"

TABLE OF CONTENTS

CHAPTER IV

CHAPTER I

INTRODUCTION

This is a private collection of heirloom artifacts from a Tingguian family whose ancestors were able to preserve and pass them down to the seventh generation owner who has great appreciation, profound admiration, and sheer pride of the culture and tradition of her heritage. It is with true love and sincere affection that this collection project is dedicated to their loving memories.

PROLOGUE

Writing about the Tingguian family collection is to express my deep appreciation to my most revered Tingguian ancestors, and to manifest my sincere thanksgiving to the phenomenal love and care of my parents especially my kind and generous father, Santiago Banganan Espiritu (the sixth generation owner of the family collection), for passing down to me the prized possession of the family. That thoughtful gesture made me the seventh generation beneficiary of the Tingguian family collection.

The collection project is an initiative of recapturing the spirit of my ancestors to make a connection with them. By using any of the pieces of the collection is feeling their presence or just like carrying the history of my Tingguian ancestry. This project is giving me sheer pride and joy for my ancestors and for the whole Tingguian tribe for their appreciation to the wonderful work of arts like the jars and other earthen wares; their way of valuing the beauty of natural gemstones such as agates and other kinds of beads and their efforts in participating and supporting the historical trade relationship that existed between the early Chinese traders and the early group of people in the northern part of the Philippines including the Tingguians of Abra. The Tingguian group involvement in the early trading was shown by their acquisition of numerous antique Chinese products in their possession from the l0th-15th century AD, which encompassed the Tang dynasty to Ming dynasty before the advent of the Spanish into the Philippine Shore in 1521.

The Chinese jars, plates, saucers, brass gongs, and ancient beads are believed to be a part of the Martaban Jars made during the Ming dynasty or even earlier. They were brought into trading by the early Chinese traders or even by the early Chinese pirates with the early people of the Northern part of the Philippines or the Cordillera Region. The dates of the jars and beads in the collection cannot be ascertained, but through stories shared by the family and informal research made, the jars in the collection are akin to the Martaban jars in their appearances, sizes, designs and colors. The three large jars in the collection are with dragon heads and the design of the dragon is inscribed around the body in two of those jars resembling the dragon jars in the Martaban jar group. The Chinese emperor dragon jars are considered prestigious and more valuable because the "Dragon" is the symbol of the emperor, who is known to be the "ruler of the universe." The dragon jars are the symbol of wealth and status among various indigenous groups in the South East Asia. The agates in the collection are similar to the Dong Son Beads like the long Carnelian Indus Valley Beads produced in India that crossed the borders of Vietnam, Cambodia, Thailand, China, and the Philippines. Beads are said to be great travelers!

Records have shown that there was an extensive trade relationship between the early Chinese traders and the early people of the northern part of the Philippines from 984 AD to the 15th century. Warm diplomatic trade relationships existed, and as such, the tribal leaders of the north made some trips to Peking (now called Beijing) to pay homage to the emperor.

The early Tingguians and the other early tribe groups in the north treasured the antique jars and antique beads profoundly. The importance and usage of these artifacts have always been reflected in their folk tales from ancient times and to their history. The antique jars were significantly used as a bride dowry to a future bride made by the family of the groom, utilized to settle disputes and applied as payments for debts. The antique beads, especially the agates, are considered "Power Stone," they were not only great adornment for the ladies to use during festivities, but the agate beads have "healing power." They were used as a protection from evil spirits and they provide stability and security. Ownership of these artifacts, in addition to vast land holdings and numerous animals, was the source of honor and prestige in the community. The owners were called the "Baknangs," the well-to-do families in the community. The history of the ancient agate beads and ancient jars are passed down from one generation to the next in the same manner as the artifact heirlooms are transferred from one hand to another in the family.

LEAVING AND KEEPING THE LEGACY

SANTIAGO BANGANAN ESPIRITU

TINGGUIAN FROM ABRA, PHILIPPINES

RETIRED SERGEANT-AT-ARMS,

HOUSE OF REPRESENTATIVES, PHILIPPINES

MERLINA ESPIRITU SALAMANCA

EDUCATIONAL SPECIALIST, U.S.A.

CERTIFIED EDUCATOR, U.S.A.

WHO ARE THE TINGGUIANS?

The Tingguians or Itnegs appeared to have traces of ancient Indonesian element and Malayan culture. When the Spanish colonized the island, they called the mountain dwellers, Tingguians. The term derived from the Malayan word "Tinggi or Tingue" which means mountain or elevated place. In the later years, the term referred solely to the inhabitants of Abra. They are likewise called "Itnegs," calling them in generalization as people from Tineg, a name of a place and important river in Abra which supplies water to neighboring provinces. The word Abra originated from the Spanish word "to open," referring to the water of the Abra river which opens a waterway to the China Sea.

The Tingguians are an indigenous group of people from Abra. The Tingguians have a culture, custom, traditions, rituals, beliefs, idiosyncracies, and ethnic values much the same as the people of the Cordillera Region, and may be with minor differences if they exist. The old Tingguians viewed that the Supreme Being was worshipped and given the same adoration as the God of Christians. According to Fay Cooper Cole, an American author of The Traditions of the Tingguians: A Study in Philippine Forklore, claimed that "Kadaklan" was the Supreme Being. However, Florencio Millare from Abra, who also traveled extensively to the places covered by Cole pointed out that "Bagatulayan" was the Ultimate Being. He just assigned some powers to Kadaklan who in some instances have exceeded the powers delegated to him. Kadaklan was called the "king of lightning" (ari ta sil-it). Kaboniyan was placed third in the rank of Tingguian heirarchical ladder of deities. Kaboniyan was a benevolent spirit. He was friendly and helpful to the Tingguians. Kaboniyan guided the Tingguians on how to live right, to pray, and to interpret omens. He communicated through mediums, or spiritual healers, the medicines and the healing procedures to be followed. He was known to have rewarded the deserving Tingguians of Agate beads and talking jars. Kaboniyan married a Tingguian. He lived with his wife in a cave with prolific plants and trees. The Tingguians always remembered Kaboniyan with gratitude and repect for the support and wonderful service that he had so kindly rendered to them. There were also other spirits with lower ranks, but they were equally appeased and respected.

To this day, the Tingguians are all Christianized. The inevitable change of time, indoctrination of religion, power of education and job opportunities had improved their social condition and their life style. The Tingguians, wherever they are, still hold on to their valued custom which is harmonious to society, because their cultural traits and beliefs are bringing them together in their relationship, their identity, and their tradition, "Kabagyan ken ugali ta Itneg."

THE ESPIRITU FAMILY

L-R Sra. Luisa (Libayan), Sra. Merlina (Mil-lie), Atty. Isidro (Sid), and Sr. Santiago (Banganan).

ATTY. ISIDRO PANDAY ESPIRITU WITH HIS SISTER

Atty. Isidro Panday Espiritu with his sister, Merlina Espiritu-Salamanca and her three grandchildren: Joshua, Christopher and Sebastian Villalta, sons of Elaine Salamanca Villalta. All college graduates from the USA went to the Philippines with their grandmother to celebrate the Death Anniversary or "Lay-og" of their great grandmother, Sra. Luisa Panday Espiritu in 2012.

SANTIAGO (BANGANAN) ESPIRITU

Santiago (Banganan, Tingguian name) Espiritu was born in Danglas, Abra, Philippines. He was the son of the late Capitan Callibag and the late Capitana Bayayog (only child of the late Capitan Luben and Capitana Awidan). He had two sisters: Concepcion (Immoy) and Tasing (Lindawan, maternal half sister). His father (Capitan Callibag) became the mayor of Danglas, Abra and in Nueva Era, Ilocos Norte (neighboring province) Philippines. Santiago continued his studies and completed his primary grades in Ilocos Norte. He was baptized and named after the governor of Ilocos Norte, Santiago Espiritu, who was a dear friend and political ally of his father.

At the age of sixteen, he started working with Don Quintin Paredes at the Paredes law office in Manila, Philippines and completed his secondary schooling while working. He pursued some business courses until he got married. He married Luisa (Libayan, Tingguian name) and they were blessed with four children: Santiago Jr. (Deceased), Isidro (Deceased), Merlina, and Violeta (Deceased). He had decided to work for the government and he gained a long successful government position. His last position was Sergeant- at- Arms, in the House of Representatives in Manila, Philippines. He held that position until his retirement, Santiago and Luisa came and lived in the U.S. in 1988, and they made ocassional visits to the Philippines. They went back home in the Philippines in 1994. Both Santiago and Luisa are now deceased.

Santiago had always been actively involved and strong supporter of Tingguian Cultural Affairs. He was one of the founders of ATCA (Abra Tingguian Cultural Affairs) in the Philippines and one of the founders/advisers of TCA (Tingguian Culture of America) in the USA. The family is very supportive to local and community activities especially to social, cultural, and educational endeavors. There is endless respect, dedication, and support of their children: Isidro, a CPA-Lawyer, and Merlina, Educational Specialist and Certified Educator in the United States.

Santiago and Luisa brought to America some of the prized possessions of the family (Tingguian heirloom artifacts) to Merlina, their only surviving daughter, who had shown early love, sincere dedication, and utmost respect to the Tingguian culture of the Philippines. Merlina is the seventh generation in line to receive those family-valued possessions.

KEEPING THE TINGGUIAN FAMILY LEGACY
CHAIN OF OWNERSHIP OF THE ARTIFACTS

7th Generation owner-Mil-lie/ MERLINA /MERLIE ESPIRITU- SALAMANCA (Daughter of Santiago).

6th Generation owner-Banganan/ SANTIAGO, AGO / ESPIRITU, only son of Capitana Bayayog and Capitan Cal-libag, an Ex-Mayor in Danglas, Abra and in Nueva Era, Ilocos Norte.

5th Generation owner-Capitana Bayayog, only daughter of Capitan Luben and Capitana Awidan, Awidan had the same name with the first owner (tocayo only).

4th Generation owner-Luben, Ex-mayor of Danglas, Abra, was the Father of Capitana Bayayog and the son of Balit.

3rd Generation owner-Balit, was the father of Capitan Luben and son of Taon. He was the third generation to own the artifacts.

2nd Generation owner-Taon, was the daughter of Awidan, the second beneficiary to the heirloom of artifacts.

1st Generation owner-Awidan, was the person that could be traced and remembered to be the first to own the artifacts.

CHAPTER II

AMAZING STORIES ABOUT THE ARTIFACTS

Amazing stories about the artifacts transcend from generation to generation where the Tingguians viewed that "Kaboniyan," the benevolent spirit, or the creator, or God, had rewarded industrious farmers and hunters whom he appreciated with talking jars and agates, hanging in branches of plants near the cave where he lived. Cabildo confirmed the story about the talking jar. He was the grandson of Magsawi, the hunter who owned the famous talking jar. He was from Patok, Peñarubia, Abra. He claimed that Magsawi had a hard time catching the eluding talking jar, but an unknown voice suggested to Magsawi how to catch the jumping, running, and talking jar. Magsawi had to kill a pig without young and offer the blood to the spirit. After Magsawi complied, he was able to catch the jar. The story spread and was extensively published. Tingguian elders were happy talking about the generosity and support of Kaboniyan to the Tingguians. There are other remarkable stories cited in the folk tales of the Tingguians. One of them was when Kaboniyan had turned the water that dropped from the bodies of the ladies taking a bath in a river into agates a long, long time ago. The Tingguians postulate that the jars or the beads were either from Kaboniyan or from their ancestors. Whatever the case may be, the stories are mysterious and enchanting!

ANTIQUE DRAGON JAR WITH FLYING DRAGON
(MAGALAO NGA NAMARKAAN TA DRAGON)

The Tingguians of Abra called this large jar the "Magalao jar." This is an ancient Chinese jar with four dragon heads below the mouth of the jar and with wavy lines. The jar has four flying dragons carved around it and with double straight and wavy lines at the lower part of the jar. The jar is a glazed stoneware resembling the Martaban "Dragon jars" produced during the Ming dynasty in the 13th - 16th century AD. The jar could be one of the vessel jars used for storage for food and water, but included in the trading. The Dragon jar is always prized higher than the other jars. There was an extensive trade relationship of the early Chinese traders with the early people of the northern part of the Philippines, the Cordillera Region consisting of (BIBAK): Benguet, Ifugao, Bontoc, Apayao, and Kalinga. Included in this group appreciating the antique jars are the Tingguians of Abra.

ANTIQUE DRAGON JAR WITH DRAGON AND PEARL DESIGN (MAGALAO NGA UWAD TA MARKA DRAGON KEN PEARLAS NA)

This jar has four dragon heads with two rows of embossed pearl-like design all around. The jar is naturally glazed stoneware like the Martaban Dragon jar made during the Ming Dynasty. There are four flying dragons engraved around the body of the jar with circular sketches at the lower base. It is believed that this jar was among those brought to the trading by the early Chinese traders. The Dragon jars are always respected and of higher value. History noted that there was an extensive trade relationship of the early Chinese traders with the early people of the northern part of the Philippines or the Cordillera Region, before the advent of the Spaniards in 1521.

ANTIQUE DRAGON JAR WITH SKETCH OF FLYING BIRD. (MARKA DRAGON A TIBOR NGA UWAD TA AGILA NA)

This is an Antique Dragon jar with four dragon heads below the mouth of the jar and incised with four flying birds around its body. It is a glazed stoneware jar similar to the Martaban jar produced during the Ming Dynasty as one of the vessel jars for storage of food and water, but included in the trading by the early Chinese traders during their trade relationship with the early people of the Northern part of the Philippines, before the arrival of the Spaniards in 1521.

YOUNG MALAYO JAR (URBON TA MALAYO TIBOR)

This jar is in the group of the most valued antique jars. The valued jar could be presented as a bride prize or as a dowry to a future bride by the groom's family. It could be used in a feud settlement and applied for debt payment. The price of this jar is equivalent to a price of several animals such as the carabao or cattle. It is believed that the ancestors of the family owner of the jar could have acquired the jar in the 10th century AD, during the Tang dynasty. The jar is smooth and beautifully glazed with a dark brown color. It has four ears below the mouth of the jar. The jar is called the "Young Malayan jar," Urbon ta Malayo tibor." This jar was probably one of the earlier products of pottery brought in the Philippines by the early Chinese traders, before the advent of the Spanish in 1521.

SAO-IT JAR (SAO-IT TIBOR)

This is a unique antique Chinese jar with a rough design of leaves painted in a glossy paint of green in the background of red brown, and with a dub of yellow to give a brighter effect and beauty to the vase. The coloring of the jar is similar to the Sancai Pottery where only three colors were used in painting the jar. The Sancai pottery was produced during the Tang Dynasty. The color scheme was called "Egg and Spinach."

MANAPIS PLATES

These three antique Chinese plates of different sizes; small, medium, and large, were used for eating, but now they are occasionally for ceremonial use and for display in the house. The plates might be a part of the Sancai pottery production, because of the use of three colors in painting, the green, brown red, and with white background.

ANTIQUE CHINESE PLATTER- INALDANAN

This is an antique platter. This kind of platter was probably brought into trading by the early Chinese traders with the early people of the northern part of the Philippines. The platter has practical and ceremonial usages. It was used for serving food, but now, the platter is used at wedding ceremonies to twirl a coin while calling relatives, friends, and guests for their monetary gifts to the newlywed. "Umay cayon, umay cayon cabagyan partis mangted ta regalo yon." Come, come relatives and friends, give your gifts to the newlywed. It is also used to put meat to offer to the spirits at rituals.

THE THREE PLATTERS – TAL-LO NGA INALDALAN

The three platters are with the same design, but with different shades of fading blue. They are of inferior quality of the colors blue and white, which was probably due to the shortage of imported cobalt. That shortage was attributed to the political instability at the time. These platters may have been produced during the Ming Dynasty in 1368-1643 AD, which was brought into the trading by the Chinese traders. The platters were used for serving foods, but now the platters are used at wedding ceremonies to twirl a coin while calling for relatives, friends and guests for monetary gifts for the couple. It is also used to put meat to offer to the spirits at rituals.

BLUE AND WHITE MANAPIS PLATE (MANAPIS NGA PURAO KEN ASUL A PINGGAN)

This medium sized plate is called "Manapis." It is a dinner plate painted with glossy blue on a white background. This is an old Chinese dinner plate used for eating, but now it is used for decoration, or as display in houses or used to put meat to offer to the spirits at rituals.

DIFFERENT ANTIQUE CHINESE PLATES(NADUMA-DUMA NGA PING-GAN)

These old Chinese plates may have been produced during the Ming dynasty in 13th-16th century AD where the production of blue and white plates were generally of inferior quality, caused by the shortage of cobalt because of unstable political condition at that time. It is believed that those plates were brought into the trading during the trade relationship of the early Chinese, with the early people of the Northern part of the Philippines, including the Tingguians of Abra. There was an extensive trade relationship of the early Chinese traders and the early people of the Northern part of the Philippines, before the arrival of the Spaniards in 1521. These plates were used for eating, but now they are used for home display or for decoration, and occasionally used at rituals to put meat for offering to the spirits.

PROVINCE OF ABRA

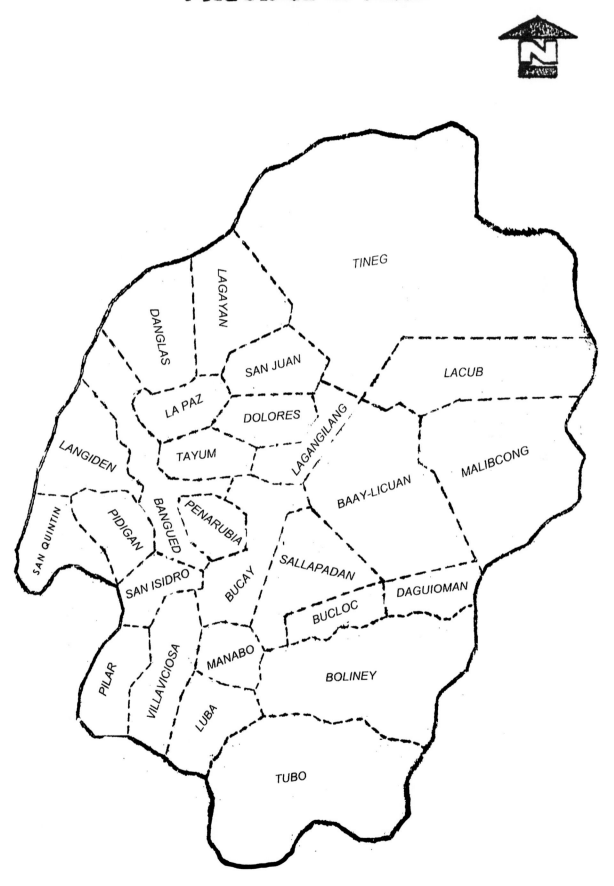

CHAPTER III

ANCIENT HEIRLOOM OF ARTIFACTS STAYED IN STYLE THEN AND NOW

**SANTIAGO AND LUISA ESPIRITU OF
DANGLAS, ABRA, PHILIPPINES**

KNOWING AND APPRECIATING AGATE

Agate is considered as a semi-precious gemstone based on its natural beauty. It is used as ornamental stone. It is a part of the quartz family, which is a variety of chalcedony. It is translucent and banded in different shades from light to darker color. Agate is a product of many years of deposits of silica from groundwater in cavities of fiery or volcanic rocks. Agate was discovered when the philosopher Theophrastus was walking along the shore of the river called Achates River in Sicily, Italy. Agate is considered as a "power stone," and agate properties relate with the energy of the earth. There are various impressions and beliefs noted by different groups at different civilizations that have bearing on what agate can do since ancient times to date. Ancient Islamic culture, wards off evil and tragedies; ancient Babylonians, dispel evil energy; ancient Egyptians, protection against natural disaster, like lightning, from thirst, and help to deliver power of speech; Persian, protect against storm. The Chinese viewpoint is more internal. The Chinese believed that agate has the following effects:

a.) Spiritual protection,

b.) Could stimulate ones strength while cleansing his mind to make space for good luck and good fortune; agate is the oldest healing and protective stone.

When the early Tingguians acquired the ancient agates from the early Chinese traders, they were most likely informed of everything about the stone. Tingguians believed and respected everything about the power stone. The stone is mysterious, and this was reinforced by their experiences with the agates from "Kaboniyan," the Tingguian mediums or spiritual healers demonstrated the importance of the power stone by wearing an agate necklace in their rituals asking for good health and good luck of a person.

Sra. Luisa Espiritu and Sra. Embelleng Castillo were using the original style of blouse called "Ringgi" made out of peña or pineapple fabric. The white rectangular wrap around skirt borded with red woven thread is known as the "Piningitan," by the Tingguian women of Abra.

Ladies from Manabo, Abra, Philippines wore their Tingguian traditional attire in attending the Death Anniversary (Lay-og) celebration for Sr. Santiago Banganan Espiritu of Danglas, Abra, Philippines.

Sra. Luisa Panday Espiritu with niece, Lorena Agcalis Andres and her sister, Maria Panday Castillo sponsored the Lay-og for the late Sr. Santiago Banganan Espiritu.

THE TINGGUIAN JEWELS
(THE PRIDE POSSESSIONS OF THE TINGGUIANS)

THE ANCIENT BANDED AGATE BEADS ENSEMBLE

This is an ancient banded agate beads ensemble: A pair of agate earrings (Aritos), two layered agate beads necklace (Gon-Gon) and with a matching bracelet (Pulseras). The ensemble is made out of ancient banded agate beads strung alternately with yellow beads and gold beads spacers. The agate beads have an incredible design of band from light to dark brown that shine in a yellowish color of honey. The color gives luster and shows more fine stripes in the translucent gemstone. The agate beads are so similar to the Dong son agates from India. The beads are spectacular. Some old Tingguians sometimes believed that beads like these are gifts from Kaboniyan or God. These beautiful beads are not for daily wear, but for special occasion as in funerals (bago-ngon), weddings (pulya), and in death anniversaries (lay-og).

AN ANCIENT 12 INCH LONG TRANSLUCENT AGATE BEADS NECKLACE

This 12 inch long necklace is alternately arranged with gold beads in single and double strands of translucent, narrower, and shorter ancient agate beads. It has a stunning flat enhancer with white wavy band making the necklace an authentic natural beauty that gets immediate attention and admiration from everyone.

SETTING OF ANCIENT BANDED AGATE BEADS INTO RING AND EARRINGS (TERNO ARITOS KEN SINGSING TA BALITOC KEN GAMENG)

The ancient agate beads are skillfully set in an 18k gold of beautiful flower design and two dangling agate beads in each of the earrings. The agate beads are in a translucent caramel base color with stripes of white and different shades of brown color, from light to darker brown, that swirl around the beads, giving the jewelry a distinctive look of true elegance.

ANCIENT BANDED AGATE BEADS NECKLACE (GON-GON)

This is a 20 inches long necklace consisting of large, medium, small, and narrow sizes of ancient banded agates. The beads are strung wonderfully with yellow beads, gold beads, and some gold overlay beads as spacers. The necklace is shown with some larger and darker brown color of banded agates, and some are with white stripes, giving a good contrast to the color of the beads. The necklace has beautiful matching earrings.

AN ANCIENT 20 INCHES LONG OPAQUE AGATE BEADS

This is a necklace with ancient opaque dark brown and smoky white agate beads. There are thirty agate beads alternately strung with ten yellow beads, seven gold beads, and four silver beads spacers. The agate beads are almost the same in sizes and colors. The necklace is completed with a delicately crafted mother of pearl enhancer.

ARMLETS (BALSAY / BATEK)

These are armlets for right and left adornment. Antique beads of different colors and sizes are carefully fastened together to form a cylindrical design and pattern to fit the forearm from the wrist to the elbow. The interlacing of antique, bright and colorful beads made this jewelry different and expensive. This style of female accessory became impractical and outmoded. They are just now a part of a souvenir or a collection of artifacts.

ANCIENT AGATE BEADS NECKLACE
WITH LARGE FLAT ENHANCER

This is a single strand necklace of ancient agate beads which were strung alternately with gold beads. It is a mixture of longer, skinnier, shorter, and translucent agate beads from light to darker brown beads with stripes of white in some of the beads. The necklace is completed by a large, flat, banded, and beautiful agate enhancer which was added by the new owner in the early 1990's. It has a matching set of earrings.

ANCIENT AGATE BEADS WITH
INDIAN DESIGN ENHANCER

Two strands of small, skinny, and narrow ancient beads alternately strung with gold filled beads are separately attached to a delicately and intricately designed gold overlay Indian enhancer with tiny gold filled trimmings. It is with matching agate bead earrings with yellow beads and gold filled silver beads.

ANCIENT AGATE BEADS HEADDRESS (APO-NGOT)

The two strands of ancient banded agate beads of different sizes were made into a headdress. The beads were strung alternately together with yellow beads, gold beads, and some gold washed beads. The length of the headdress is long enough to fit the head of the wearer. The headdress is occasionally used in festivities such as in death anniversaries (lay-og), in funerals (bago-ngon), and other cultural ceremonies. The Tingguian ladies enjoy wearing this piece of jewelry because it signifies respect and distinctive fashion of the Tingguian ladies.

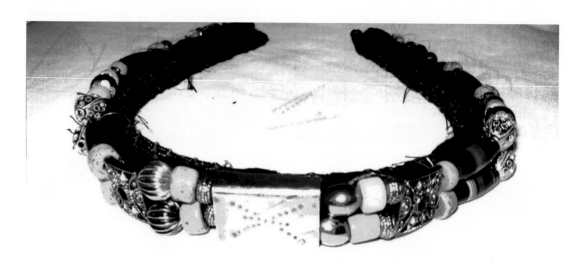

AGATE AND YELLOW BEADS HEADDRESS
IN A HEADBAND (AMBOSAO)

This is another kind of headdress where two strands of ancient agate beads, yellow beads, and gold filled beads are securely attached to a headband for easier and faster placement on the head, which is adjustable to fit the head of the wearer.

CORAL BEADS NECKLACE

The necklace is 25 inches long of coral beads. Five coral beads are strung alternately with gold beads and silver beads. The large round gold bead is found at the middle of the necklace, followed by two gold medium size beads in between five coral beads. The sequence is continued by smaller gold and silver beads until the end. The necklace has matching earrings with one round gold bead, yellow bead, and two coral beads in each pair of the earrings.

CARNELIAN BEADS MADE INTO CONVERTIBLE HEADDRESS AND NECKLACE

The headdress was creatively designed so that for every three carnelian beads, a gold overlay bead, and two pink venetian glass beads, were alternately strung. The front view was adorned with three round brass enhancers. This style could be used as a necklace or as a headdress.

CORAL AND PEARL BEADS NECKLACE
WITH INDIAN BRASS ENHANCER

This necklace is 20 inches coral and pearl. This 20 inch necklace is made of coral and pearl beads. The coral, pearl, gold, and silver beads are alternately arranged in two single strands. The strands are separately and securely attached to an amazing and delicately designed Indian brass enhancer and small shiny round trimmings, which were added for beauty and value. It has a coordinating pair of earrings.

CORAL HEADDRESS (APO-NGOT)

This is another style of headdress. It is a longer strand of antique coral, agate, yellow beads, and silver spacers. This style is used by older women with long hair. They will follow the figure eight formation, where the woman will gather her long hair to a ponytail. One hand will hold the hair, while the other hand will slide the strand of agates through the ponytail and twist it to form the figure eight and make some adjustments to fit the head. The ponytail will be divided in half to be tacked into the sides of the beads until the hair is safely fastened with the beads in the head. For additional adornment, they can accent the front view with pieces of gold, such as gold flower pins or other motifs for beauty.

ANCIENT, BANDED, AND DARKER
COLOR AGATE BEADS

This is a 12 inch necklace of ancient banded agate beads in a single strand. The larger beads have some chips in the ends as part of "wear and tear." It is matched with earrings.

CHAPTER IV

Atty. Sid Panday Espiritu with his mother Luisa Panday Espiritu,
and aunts; Belen Santos and Maria Castillo.

I AM A TINGGUIAN

I am a Tingguian, and I am proud to be one.

Everywhere I go, I am still the same one.

National or International, Tingguians are found.

We are all the products of long struggles to exist as one.

Our ancestors stood and fought for the protection and preservation of our mores.

Younger generations should pursue the continuation of those traditions from long time ago.

Good luck to all of us.

May we keep in touch to hear that our heritage is still intact.

Merlina Espiritu-Salamanca, With love

ACCESSORIES DURING THE SPANISH TIME

SOME UNIQUE JEWELRY STYLES FASHIONED DURING THE COLONIAL TIMES

When the Spaniards colonized the Philippines in 1521, they left some remarkable imprints that have been embedded into the Filipino culture. The fashion of wearing jewels is one of them. Delicate and intricate designs of male and female accessories were introduced such as rings, earrings, bracelets, combs, male baton, and buttons made of gold or silver, and other gold plated metals. The use of Tamborin or tambourine necklace for ladies was in high fashion during the colonial time that complemented the use of the well known Maria Clara style gown which was popularized by the legendary Maria Clara of the Philippines. Tamborin necklace is a beautiful piece of Filipino jewelry patterned after the use of a rosary as a necklace where the crucifix was later replaced by creative goldsmiths in using the motif of nature, like flowers and leaves. The handmade beads were formed by the use of spool or frame in guiding a needle like an instrument in looping and twirling of fine thread-like wire giving these beads the name tambourine from tambour, the frame used in needle work.

TAMBOURINE NECKLACE WITH EARRINGS

This is a gold "Tambourine or Tamborin" necklace with large enhancer and beads designed and handmade in tambour. It is matched with beautiful gold earrings.

TAMBORIN ENSEMBLE

This set of a Tamborin necklace was from Sra. Luisa Panday Espiritu (mother of the Merlina). The Tamborin set was in gold overlay in silver. The set consists of two combs, earrings, ring, bracelet, and the necklace.

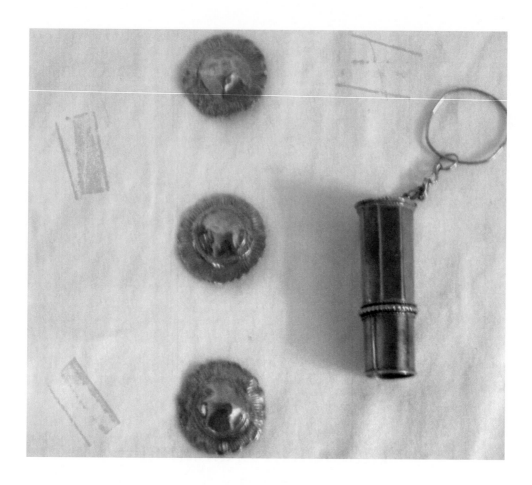

GOLD BUTTONS (BOTONES) AND A GOLD CANE HOLDER (SONGCOP TA BASTON)

Three gold buttons were used to accentuate a headdress or used as buttons for male or female shirts.

The gold cane cap holder or "Baston" cap was fashioned by the male Spaniards and Filipinos to hold their skinny cane or 'baston'as part of their social accessories. Filipino men are no longer using the "Baston." The baston cap was used by the great grandfather of the author (Merlina Espiritu Salamanca) when he was using baston during his administration as mayor of Danglas, Abra, Philippines.

TWO GOLD COMBS IN CARABAO HORN FRAME

These are two combs made out of Carabao horn. The comb with the missing teeth is adorned with decorative 14 carat gold. The other comb is decorated with a flower design of 18 carat gold. The comb is used as an adornment to the head or to hold the hair of the ladies. It is also worn to compliment their traditional attire.

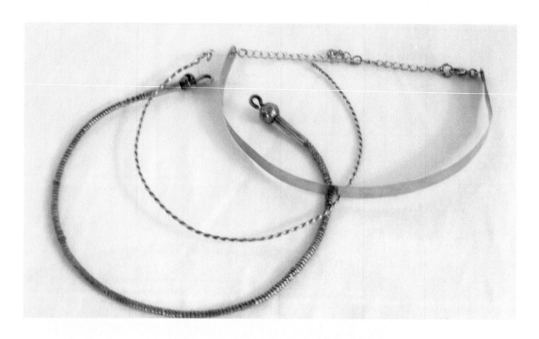

GOLD CHOKERS

These are three different styles of gold chokers (gon-gon): one skinny and twisted choker, the second one is flat and narrow, and the third one is coarsely boarded all around and it is called the "lizard"or the "banias." The Tingguian ladies love to wear chokers or necklaces in layers at festivities.

EPILOGUE

Working with the TINGGUIAN FAMILY COLLECTION project has given me the opportunity to reflect upon the history of my roots, (The Tingguians of Abra, Philippines), with so much to learn along the way, aside from the knowledge acquired while growing up, and stories heard from family members and elders in the Tingguian community. It is so fascinating to know that countries back then had been globally interconnected through the power of trade as shown by the acquisition of the early Tingguians of jars, beads, clothes, gongs, and other goods not made in the Philippines, but they are most likely from other countries like India, Cambodia, Japan, Thailand, Indonesia, Malaysia, and China. The universal admiration for beautiful works of art and appreciation of natural gemstones inspired people to have them. Sharing the pictures in the collection and their history would show that trade alliance among nations was the foundation of better understanding, and a means for excellent communication and interactions for peaceful relationships of many cultures.

ACKNOWLEDGMENT AND DEDICATION

This is to express my heartfelt thanks to my friends, relatives and brother, Atty. Isidro Panday Espiritu, who stood behind me and have supported this project by providing information and tremendous encouragement in writing this book.

I dedicate with great affection this book in the memory of my Tingguian ancestors, family, parents, Luisa and Santiago Espiritu. I would especially like to thank my father, who preserved the Tingguian relics as discussed in the book and had lovingly and generously given them to me. I also sincerely appreciate my children: Michael and Elaine and her three sons: Joshua, Kristofer, and Sebastian for inspiring me in the completion of this project.

GLOSSARY

ABRA- name of a province of the Philippines. Spanish word, to open.

AMBUSAO- short style of Tingguian headdress

APONGOT- Tingguian headdress, short or long style

ARITOS- earrings

BAGATULAYAN- GOD OR CREATOR

BAGONGON- funeral rites

BAKNANG- rich or wealthy

BALITOC- gold

BALSAY- armlet made of different beads with different colors

BASTON- cane

BATEK- armlet made of beads and it could also mean tattoo

BITIN- enhancer

BOTONES- buttons

CAPITAN- former mayor or ex-mayor

CAPITANA- wife of former mayor or wife of ex-mayor

CORALES- coral beads

GAMENG- beads

ITNEG-I Malayan word meaning from, Tineg, it is a name of a municipality or river in Abra, Philippines. Tingguians are alternately called ITNEGS.

KABAGYAN- relatives

KABONIYAN- GOD or the Creator

KADAKLAN- God, according to Fay Cooper Cole

LAY-OG- celebration of Death Anniversary

MAGALAO- large jar

MANAPIS- type of plate

PERLAS- pearl

PING-GAN / PINGGAN- plate

PLATO- plate

PULSERAS- bracelet

SING-SING- ring

SUNGCOP- cap

TAMBOURINE OR TAMBORIN- necklace where beads were made from spool or frame called tambour. Necklace modeled from the rosary where the crucifix was changed to the natures motif like flowers and leaves. This style of necklace was popular during the Spanish period in the Philippines.

BIBLIOGRAPHY

An Encyclopedia Guide. Genuine Gemstone Limited, 2012.

Bennet, Steve. The little Book of Gemstone Company Limited, 2002.

Cole, Fay Cooper. The Tradition of the Tingguians. Field Museum of Natural History publication 180. Anthropological Series. Vol. X1V No. Chicago, 1915.

Dozier, P. Edward. Mountain Arbiters. The Changing life of Philippine Hill People. The University of Arizona, 1966.

Dozier, P. Scott. The Kalinga of Northern Luzon, Philippines, 1957.

Dueppen, Stephen. Asian Perspective Vol. 52 No. 1. University of Hawaii. Asst. Professor in the Dept. of Anthropology at the University of Oregon. Oregon, U.S.A., 2014.

Dumagat, Fay. "The Ways of the Itnegs". Filipino Heritage Vol. 6 Philippines: Lahing Pilipino Publishing, Inc., 1978.

Nid, Anima. Social Life and Custom of a Culture. Omar Publication. Laloma Q.C., Philippines, 1982.

Scott, Henry William. Discovery of the Igorots. Spanish Contact with the Pagans of the Northern Luzon, Philippines, 1974.

Weygen, Louise C. Philian. Rituals of Abra from the Philippines. Tingguian Abra Rituals. Posted by: Philouise on August 25, 2009.

Zaide F. Gregorio. Philippine History Corrected Edition. Published by National Book Store, 1984 & 1987.

ORAL ACCOUNTS

Espiritu, Banganan Santiago. Retired Sgt.-At-Arms, House of Representatives Philippines. (6th generation Owner of the collection of Artifacts), Oral Accounts on the Ownership of Artifacts, History and Tradition of the Tingguians.

Espiritu, Panday Isidro. CPA-Lawyer (Brother of Merlina), Oral Accounts on History and Tradition of the Tingguians.

Lejos, Marcelina. Community Elder. Oral Accounts on Ownership of the Artifacts, History and Tradition.

Pascua, Valeriano. Ex-Vice Mayor of Danglas, Philippines. Oral Accounts on Ownership, History and Tradition of the Tingguians.

INTERNET SOURCES

Ancient Bead.com

https://en.wikipedia.orgwiki/chinese-dragon

ISTphilippines.com

AUTHOR'S PROFILE

Merlina Espiritu-Salamanca was born and raised in Danglas, Abra, Philippines. Both parents are Tingguians. She was married to Dr. Manuel V. Salamanca of Mayantoc, Tarlac, Philippines. Dr. Salamanca came to America to work and for medical training. Merlina and five months old daughter, Elaine followed. The couple are blessed with two children: Michael Salamanca and Merlyn Elaine S. Villalta. Merlina has three loving grandchildren: Joshua, Christopher, and Sebastian Villalta.

Education in the Philippines: Bachelor of Laws Degree (LL.B.),1963, Manuel L. Quezon University, Manila, Philippines.

Education in U.S.A.: Bachelor of Arts, 1980; Master of Education Social Studies, 1986; Master of Education in Behavior Disorders, 1988, Columbus College (CSU), Columbus, Georgia; Educational Specialist Degree in Social Studies, 1991; Educational Specialist Degree in Behavior Disorder, 1992; Troy State University, Phenix City, Alabama. T-6 certification in Social Studies, Behavior Disorder and Political Science, State of Georgia.

Scholastic honors:

Awardee-CNI (Commission on National Integration) Scholarship, Philippines, 1960-1963.

Kappa Delta Pi-An International Honor Society in Education (1991- to date) Troy State University.

Phi Beta Delta-Honor Society for International Scholars (2016 to date) Columbus State University.

Zeta Phi Beta Sorority, Inc. Epsilon Eta Zeta Chapter "Finer Womanhood/Community Pearl."

Member: Mayor's Commission on Unity, Diversity and Prosperity.

Commission on International Relations and Cultural Liaison Encounter, (CIRCLE).

Author: A Look At Asian-Pacific Rim Culture, Language, Customs and History in Columbus, Georgia.

Tingguian Affairs-Magazine of Traditions and Experiences.

Former regional correspondent writer for the Heritage Magazine.

Former President of American Association of American Association of University Women, 1989-91.

Former founder and president of Club Filipino of Columbus, Georgia.

Board of Director (member) Tingguian Culture of America.

Founder and president of International Network of Columbus, Georgia.

Retired educator at Muscogee County School District (2005).

Member-Muscogee County Educators Association (2005-to date).

Member-Georgia Educators Association (2005-to date).

MERLINA ESPIRITU-SALAMANCA, LL.B., Ed.S.

Merlina Espiritu- Salamanca was born and raised in the Philippines. She is the third child of the four children of Santiago and Luisa Espiritu, both deceased so as her younger sister, Violeta Espiritu Castillo. She and her brother Isidro, a CPA, finished their Bachelor of Laws Degree from the same university, Manuel L. Quezon University in Manila, Philippines. Merlina was a recipient of full scholarship under the Commission on National Integration (CNI) a government Program of the Philippines. She was married to the late Dr. Manuel Valdez Salamanca of Mayantoc, Tarlac, Philippines. They are blessed with two wonderful children, Elaine and Michael. They have three loving grandchildren: Joshua, Kristofer, and Sebastian. Her husband joined the exodus of medical professionals in July 1969 who came to the United States for employment and for medical training. Merlina followed him with her five month old daughter in January, 1970.

Merlina and the family had decided to moved to Columbus, Georgia from Cleveland, Ohio where her husband completed his Internship and Residency from St. John Hospital and passed the Medical Board Exam to practice Medicine in the United States. Her husband was hired as Medical Staff at the VA Medical Center in Tuskegee, Alabama.

Merlina received her second Bachelors degree in Political Science and her Masters in Education at Columbus College then, now the Columbus State University. She has earned a Specialist Degree in Education from Troy State University where she was inducted as a member of KAPPA DELTA PI, an International Honor Society in Education. In 2016, she was made Honorary Member Inductee to the Delta Nu Chapter of Phi Beta Delta, an Honor Society for International Scholars by Columbus State University. Merlina has served as Legal Researcher in the Philippines as well as in the United States. She was a long time educator in the Muscogee County School System. Merlina played a central role in advocating for an internationally diverse Columbus and a city that welcomes its International guests and residents. She was a member of the Mayor's commission on Unity, Diversity, and Prosperity and had served as a Chair of the Entertainment Program of the International Festival in Columbus. She is still a member of the Commission and a member of the CIRCLE, Commission on International Relations and Cultural Liaison Encounter, an elite group of community leaders working with Columbus State

University and International Network in welcoming the students from Kiryu, Japan, the Sister city of Columbus, Georgia.

Mrs. Salamanca is the founding president of the International Network of Columbus. The organization advocates for inclusivity in the community, enhance education where she worked very closely with the late Lonnie Jackson in support of his tutorial program, and participated in the MLK Celebration Program. The late Mr. Lonnie Jackson helped the International Network in welcoming and sponsoring picnics at CSU in entertaining the students from Kiryu, Japan. Currently, the International Network is in partnership with Columbus State University in sponsoring and hosting activities for the International Students and in awarding scholarship to a deserving International Students of Columbus State University.

APPRECIATING AND SUPPORTING GLOBAL CULTURAL AWARENESS

Printed in the United States
by Baker & Taylor Publisher Services